The Hunting Party

Patrick Playter Hartigan

Double Movement Publications

Design, production, and illustration by Patrick Playter Hartigan

Cover Illustration: *Field 10,* 2014, oil stick on paper, by Patrick Playter Hartigan

Double Movement Publications
Patrick Playter Hartigan
2239 SE 47th Avenue
Portland, Oregon, 97215

for Jackson Thoreau

The Hunting Party

We are putting background
to the side, skirting the
cherry blossom, closeting
ship and shoe. We are one
kind and one happiness, a
natural assignment, a red
thing and a blue thing on
a bed of green. We sign &
signet, blush and scurry.
Barely the words escaping
the mouth, we do this new

It is a closeted array, the sun,
stars, and moon. Then some space
and air, then people educated to
relate a then and now. Then this
interested, patient crowd. Where
can you find such peace? Forests
settle and turn an ear. Mountain
and ocean still. All listening -
all perfectly available or awake

Everything I have is lost to me,
or close to another. I would let
more loose if I thought it would
help. Help what. Help when. Help
the children of astronomers, the
undocumented - the roving ones -
free of concern or advice. Sharp
little leaves, pale and tempered
and on the verge of organization

Nothing shades this world. No one
can take our pulse or prevaricate
concerning us. Naked stems remain
stems. All circus acts intact. We
are not first nor last nor are we
in between. Nothing was true when
I drew you near, and I will leave
you as I found you - a flattering
hope. In the dawn's working light
where troops and huts line up - I
speak to a purpose - I flick dust

All for the sake of gladiolas and
old brown shoes, the trial of the
century, a spinning cinnamon mess
trotted out with uncle geriatrics

Little Edmund steps to the side a
concrete lion companion in a rain
pouring from a battleship sky and
maze of glass-walled coffee shops

If trust is true the old man went
to the back of the cave reemerged
if trust is true how might you be
truth scratch scratch untrusting?

Long flowers went out of the dirt
purple & yellow-bronze scissoring
sheathed in sleeve-like armorings
they cleared the air of our thief

I was one alone, I am sure of it,
watching little girls pouring out
across the green lawn like puzzle
pieces from Catholic school buses

From oh spiraling bounty escaping
this cliffside retreats of wooden
priests, an indenturing broadcast
shook even over the unrisen dough

Bicycle wheel circumstance, their
looks and humming evenness, relax
and patter happy-drop the cooling
thrift for which and airless slop

Edmund one day link in hand, then
another then another a chain of a
sort, a chain indeed, we stop and
stop chain of considerable length

All the things of every type, and
all of time in stops and starts -
and each and every water drop, or
how he bounds and drifts together

The early morning editions had it
right putting up tent poles while
others shaving dimes falling head
over heel for petals in ones hand

In brass trumpets flowers of spun
glass, a dainty hand reaching in,
sounds of marching, celebration -
cart wheels, ice cream in the air

The outward gaze directed by self
captures familiar formations like
a lake collects water drops spoke
the old man poking at an old fire

Something new's available but you
are not the same as were the same
as evening drawn across a woman's
face like a vast and silken blade

For small projects a license will
not be necessary, while precedent
must abide the tranquil rose cast
to console our imaginary dolphins

That was morning when Edmund woke
and night when Edmund recalled my
manners and my tipping hat when I
bent to receive the morning paper

That was easy thievery - that and
speaking it to oneself, hardly an
admission to stir the waters, and
less an admission than concession

& just like June he came around a
lot gifting thus the outward gaze
like daisies strung together in a
noosen silhouette of my September

I am almost finished, said an old
soul to the vampire - I am almost
finished, mercy of close finishes
- No (Edmund) speaking to a phone

From within and through the white
doors shuttered to the sun floats
the cellophane minister gesturing
softly, birds of paradise swaying

Edmund angling insinuates himself
into the parade ground flung away
from a white palace, a cautionary
litter limned by golden standards

In a block of houses women old or
new collect by circumstance these
& that wars or traffic & typhoons
the men or conversation gone away

I have visited the old man says a
young woman Shyla whose limbs you
say are silken if gold would flow
as silk ripples to a casual touch

A plate in hand with more to come
wending the path solid & gingerly
this twice-widowed aunt Coripas -
no good will come of solitary men

An unscheduled breeze pushes at a
solitary window shade of bamboo -
species surrendered to function -
the moon also is solitary (Shyla)

If words were only sand, what sad
tragedy all substance enslaved or
no words lost - muses the village
cat and her asymmetrical glancing

More sand and more of nothing and
sand then nothing and sand what a
harmony sadness assassinating the
song who sought by accompaniments

An era of quoted terms and wander
for quotients thought Edmund lost
particulates our all-encompassing
parental theories trailing behind

A man at a cart adjusts this ring
of a finger & the ring of another
that the world rights in a moment
perfect that time should disperse

Symphony of green whose heart the
continents battle over little one
trumpet's dying note filtering to
hear but a market women's fingers

as they drum and wrap and startle
and speak and push and settle and
balance and clear or call then to
scatter the children drawing near

Shyla has digitized the day, thus
school and errands eradicate what
terms expose themselves for loose
vestiges of closeting categorical

Every blade of grass is unbounded
by assumptions of the lawn, every
bottle cap or firefly a harbinger
of game-show sharp constellations

You've got guts kid (the old man)
and a heavy brow for fighting but
this is neither time nor place if
words would vibrate at difference

Sad satellite - cresting the hill
a saffron-draped figure, trudging
Edmund's gaze sun-struck as Shyla
weaves against the pilgrim floods

I am alert to you, the green eyes
and various moods, teachable this
transparency, stalwart, caught on
fire and captured black & white -

Lost to nothing, lost to no one -
child of light, the shadow of all
things - an anticipatory hum, the
glass unbroken sailing in the air

...my silence from applause, blue
tufts of knittable stuff shredded
day cast over an amnesiatic field
set and positioned by silver pins

Do you remember work? We remember
putting it aside. Arithmetic said
as much in a notable conversation
conducted under those heavy bells

Edmund found his place. Unbeknown
and unrequited, unfettered nearly
undone he certifies a mental note
to look it up. So, the vast ocean

curling into itself, a sleep cold
and complete, our heads on pillow
of black rock still sharp, bright
- unreformed - a din of suffering

A cry ascends, reconnoiters, then
failing to locate a pen, stuffs a
notebook back again, shrugs brack
& frame and plunges just the same

Shyla collecting sticks. Shyla at
a vocation. Dull children enliven
a street bright with banners hung
ages past by an adoration pioneer

So, we have history, or what some
in the news hold at arm's length,
acclaiming properties soever like
love, liquid and gas, and fertile

I am not the same as you she said
- all doubt removed; I am just as
once I said to be, said he, whose
muscles bunched in unspoken humor

For over the castle wave of green
winds, and over the world streams
of broken banners, and over ocean
or playgrounds sound trumpet clay

I have, it must be admitted, made
improvements, said the old man. I
have, let's allow, done something
with the place, spoken to a night

Time does not pass for nothing, a
mention should be made, or throat
cleared, for the entrance of such
as were not purported anticipated

Ponder on bells *scratch scratch*
a thing to one purpose, closed or
open, end by end, a clapper to of
the purpose. Let us eat - said he

Such is news that no one observes
in love. At every opportunity the
silver pins shiver, thrilling the
peopled carpet, an undreamt music

What else is true? Little girls &
their names. Edmund took up space
as making his way to the balcony,
amphibian at variance with lilies

The chrome world, a perfect world
for the presenter, whose name one
appends, hear that if you would O
ears of dust - chants the old man

You can call hope your own, mate,
but she's no invention. One would
not mind a bit of glass about the
place, some color maybe companion

Shyla freed from crowds, Shyla at
the historical ruins. Evenings at
the library. Twice-regular church
and reservating at the laundromat

A top-down assemblage. Silenced -
and building. Line joined to line
- paragraph to scenic route - the
background recordations and white

substances too hardened overnight
now platforms, little gifts, line
to silhouette, name to flower, my
name to efforts no one can recall

whose efforts no one can reclaim.
All for all, spoken by the family
patriarch parked at the fountain,
one of two hundred aflow that day

in salutary rivers. Even so birds
appeared toxic to peace, thruddle
of pipe-stem the pipping playplay
- but more, as constructing aside

The sky confused by these details
- pippip - the fountain veritable
oasisish provided limbed flutters
& bright stockings such disrepair

Oh, I have read many, many books.
Books about you, and yours, and a
variety concerning theirs and the
dead, the dearly sung departables

Election drawing close & bothered
to check his watch who stopt dear
ages past don't you know simpling
delaying standingoutingishly - he

Patrons we are standing for years
on the backs of the hairless. Age
for age the feathers of a cap are
nothing to the long slowing, kiss

From out of out, then into in. As
from as of, then such, or send. A
one not his, not when, quarreling
- a flower, swapped out for a pen

You get too involved. You need to
relax. What's wrong with you. Can
I get an Amen. What's the deal. I
have a lot on my plate. Check it.

Red is not the color red. I don't
mean it's the word - I am so busy
right now! I have a family church
a serious job. Stop bothering me!

Shyla, and evening announced as a
breeze, gentle spray, mathematics
of a place & a purpose. Home. The
mention spelling the indifference

We gave up symptomatic, we and an
army. It was like pushing against
natural confetti. Their craze was
free as sin, violently plateauing

Little Edmund at a perch, ironing
out the wrinkles in his arms. The
day had been better than it cared
to admit (Edmund to ball of yarn)

Once when the world was young and
you had not confessed to anything
for all was possible or clear and
the birds too drifted as cherries

drift, for those who have one eye
on the horizon whites and another
for receding blues - just for one
Saturday - a quick spin around it

*

I am not the same anymore. I do not carry
those labels. I have not been sanitized &
I have not forgotten how to tie. If these
words do not suffice: proof. We do not go
about sitting on others' hands. We do not
swear like that. Juniper berries. For the
work a penny of thought: the work. He was
travel coupon road grade. The best and we
mean the best looking berries came a long
way with their adirondack electric chairs

*

www.ingramcontent.com/pod-product-compliance
Lightning Source LLC
Chambersburg PA
CBHW031336040426
42443CB00005B/372